DOWNHILL SKIING

BY KARA L. LAUGHLIN

The Child's World®
childsworld.com

Published by The Child's World®
1980 Lookout Drive • Mankato, MN 56003-1705
800-599-READ • www.childsworld.com

ACKNOWLEDGMENTS
The Child's World®: Mary Swensen, Publishing Director
The Design Lab: Design
Heidi Hogg: Editing
Sarah M. Miller: Editing

PHOTO CREDITS
© Alex Egorov/Shutterstock.com: 19; Brocreative/Shutterstock.
com: 15; dolomite-summits/Shutterstock.com: 2-3; ER_09/
Shutterstock.com: 4; gorillaimages/Shutterstock.com: cover, 1, 7,
20; iofoto/Shutterstock.com: 12-13; Morten Normann Almeland/
Shutterstock.com: 16; Sergey Novikov/Shutterstock.com: 8-9;
Vova Shevchuk/Shutterstock.com: 10-11

ISBN: 9781503807747
LCCN: 2015958120

Printed in the United States of America
Mankato, MN
June, 2016
PA02300

TABLE OF CONTENTS

Time to Ski!

Zip up your coat. Grab your gloves. It is time to go downhill skiing! Downhill skiing is also called **Alpine skiing**. It is a lot of fun!

Fast Fact!
Downhill skiing has been around since the 1850s.

Equipment

Downhill skiers need skis, boots, **bindings**, and poles. The bindings keep ski boots attached to the skis. Poles help with turns and balance.

Downhill skis are long and flat. This makes them fast on the snow.

Fast Fact!
The word "ski" comes from a Norwegian word for "wood."

7

Ski Lifts

It is hard to climb in skis. A **ski lift** will take you up the mountain. Some lifts carry skiers high above the snow. Others tow the skiers from the ground. Some push the skier. Some pull. But all ski lifts have the same job—they get skiers up the hill.

Fast Fact!
The United States, France, and Austria each have about 3,000 ski lifts.

Making Snow

No snow? No problem. **Ski resorts** use **snow machines** to make snow. Snow machines blow a mist of water up in the air. As it falls, the mist freezes. It is snow when it hits the ground.

Fast Fact!
Forty states in the United States have ski resorts.

Circles, Squares, and Diamonds

Time to ski down the **slope**! Skiers use a code to find slopes to match their skills. A green circle means easy. A blue square means medium-hard. A black diamond means difficult. More diamonds means a slope is even harder to ski.

Fast Fact!
The first recorded skiing race happened in Sweden in 1879.

Pika's Traverse
To Roundhouse Lodge
To Harmony Ridge

easier

Sun Bowl

most difficult

Harmony Chair

13

Slowing and Stopping

Skiers zigzag down the slope. This helps control their speed. To slow down or stop, skiers can push their skis out and bend their knees. This is called **snowplowing**.

Fast Fact!

An Italian man named Simone Origone holds the skiing speed record: 156.83 miles (252.4 kilometers) per hour.

Ski Jumping

Some skiers like jumping. They ski down a special ramp called an **inrun**. The ramp curves up at the end. It sends them into the air. Then they stretch out flat and soar! They are trying to stay in the air for as long as they can.

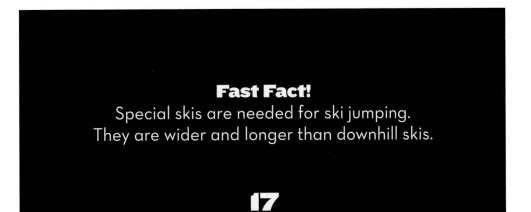

Fast Fact!
Special skis are needed for ski jumping.
They are wider and longer than downhill skis.

17

Moguls

Some people ski **moguls**. Moguls are hard bumps of snow. Some skiers zip around them. Others use them to do tricks.

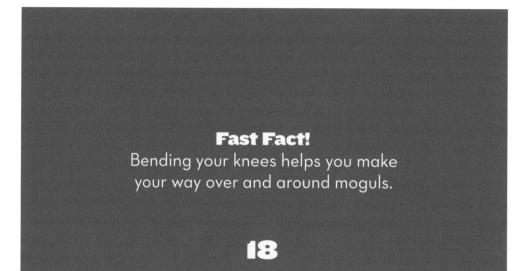

Fast Fact!
Bending your knees helps you make your way over and around moguls.

All skiers have these common goals—they want to make it down the trail. They do not want to fall. They want to have fun!

At the bottom of the hill, it is decision time. One more **run**? Or warm up in the **lodge**?

Fast Fact!
Downhill skiing has been an Olympic event since 1936.

Glossary

Alpine skiing (AL-pine SKEE-ing): Another name for downhill skiing is Alpine skiing.

bindings (BYND-ings): The places where ski boots clip into skis are called bindings.

inrun (IN-run): A ski jump. An inrun curves up at the end to launch a skier into the air.

lodge (LOJ): A building in a ski resort at the bottom of the trails. It is a place to warm up between ski runs.

moguls (MOH-guls): Hard bumps of snow on the ski slope are called moguls.

run (RUN): A run is a trip down a ski trail.

ski lift (SKEE LIFT): A ski lift is a machine that takes a skier up a mountain.

ski resorts (SKEE ree-ZORTS): Places to go downhill skiing. Some ski resorts also have rooms to stay in and places to eat.

slope (SLOHP): A trail for skiers is called a slope.

snow machines (SNOH muh-SHEENS): Machines that make snow with water droplets are called snow machines.

snowplowing (SNOH-plow-ing): A way of slowing down or stopping on skis. Skiers bend their knees and push out.

To Learn More

In the Library

Catel, Patrick. *Skiing*. Mankato, MN: Raintree, 2014.

Teitelbaum, Michael. *Skiing*. Ann Arbor, MI: Cherry Lake, 2008.

Van Dusen, Chris. *Learning to Ski with Mr. Magee.* San Francisco, CA: Chronicle Books, 2010.

On the Web

Visit our Web site for links about downhill skiing: **childsworld.com/links**

Note to Parents, Teachers, and Librarians: We routinely verify our Web links to make sure they are safe and active sites. So encourage your readers to check them out!

Index

About the Author

Kara L. Laughlin is an artist and writer who lives in Virginia with her husband, three kids, two guinea pigs, and a dog. She is the author of two dozen nonfiction books for kids.